Mr. Bunny's Guide to ActiveX

by

Carlton Egremont III

Mr. Bunny's Guide to ActiveX

Published by
Carlton Egremont III
ce3@mrbunny.com
Web: http://www.mrbunny.com

Printed in the United States of America
All trademarks referenced herein are the property of their respective owners.

ISBN 0-201-48536-2
Fine print: Copyright 1998 Addison Wesley Longman. All rights reserved.

License Agreement

By opening this book ("THE PRODUCT") you are agreeing to the following terms and conditions. This End-Reader License Agreement ("ERLA") is a legal agreement between you (an individual or single entity) and Mr. Bunny (a talking rabbit). If you do not agree to be bound by this agreement then you must close THE PRODUCT immediately and return the unread portion to Farmer Jake's back porch.

The ERLA grants you the following rights:

a) **Use of Product.** Mr. Bunny grants you a nonexclusive right to read THE PRODUCT in any room of your home or office, or in any other location providing sufficient light. You may not read more than one copy of this book at exactly the same time, since that would be impossible.

b) **Copies.** You may not make copies of THE PRODUCT except insofar as you are not caught.

c) **Storage.** You may store or install THE PRODUCT on a storage device, such as a nice maple bookcase, used only to store other books, knickknacks, and miscellaneous clutter, provided the device is not networked to any external bookcases. You must acquire and dedicate a license for each device on which THE PRODUCT is stored. Such license is automatically granted by placing THE PRODUCT on the shelf.

d) **Sample code.** Mr. Bunny grants the right to use and modify any portions of THE PRODUCT identified as sample code ("SAMPLE CODE") for the sole purpose of designing, developing, and testing your software, and crashing Visual Basic, provided that all SAMPLE CODE is clearly identified as such in your comments, and that full credit is given to Mr. Bunny on all of your product dialogs, splash screens, manuals, and promotional materials. Or not.

e) **Redistribution.** Mr. Bunny grants you the right to verbally redistribute any portion of THE PRODUCT to friends, family, coworkers, and unwitting elevator passengers, provided that you do not spoil any surprises. Mr. Bunny further grants the right to distribute THE PRODUCT as a gift, provided such gift is properly wrapped and an appropriate acknowledgment is received. THE PRODUCT may also be freely loaned to others; however, it must be returned in a timely fashion.

Credits

Technical Editor
Gary Swanberg

Non-technical Editor
Sean Welch

Illustrations
Steve Francis

Additional Illustrations
Jeremy Jacoby (age 6)
Adam Jacoby (age 9)
Barny Eggwars (age 44)

Pixel Tweaking
Randy Swanberg

Typesetting
mikeh

Author's Therapist
Nancy Newport, M.S., L.M.H.C.

Author's Mother
Mom

Consultant on Women's Issues
Mrs. Carlton Egremont III

Visit Our Web Site!
http://www.mrbunny.com

Table of Contents

Acknowledgments

Thanks.

Foreword

Well hello. I presume you've just picked up a book called *Mr. Bunny's Guide to ActiveX* and started to read the foreword. Good for you.

And what a coincidence, because I've just opened a pack of legal pads and started to write the very same foreword. Between the two of us we have collapsed time. What a team! Now tell me what I wrote next because I'm stuck.

Okay, at this point you've probably got a lot of questions. Why a talking rabbit? Who is Carlton Egremont III? Has anybody seen me reading this?

Let me address at least some of these questions.

I've known Carlton most of my life. He has always been a bit different, and has somehow always drawn me into his crazy schemes. As teenagers we ran a summer dog painting business. He'd apply the broad strokes and I'd do the trim. But Carlton took even this simple idea to extremes. One summer we had to paint a St. Bernard. The dog had an impressive southern exposure, and on a whim Carlton decided to produce a mural depicting scenes of inner city life contrasted with a patent drawing for an improved vacuum pump. Sam (the St. Bernard) didn't seem to mind, but Sam's owner turned out to be an art critic. We received terrible reviews, and had to close up shop.

Then there was Carlton's idea for fireproof ink. He figured it was perfect for people who burned their junk mail; the paper would burn but the ink would remain. Somehow Carlton thought folks would like to clean out their fireplace ashes and see "You May Already Be a Winner."

And one year I actually helped him train seeing-eye fish for blind scuba divers. The man can talk me into anything.

Still, when Carlton asked me to help with a book about ActiveX, I was hesitant. Carlton knows nothing about ActiveX. He knows little about computers. I can't even imagine where he heard the term ActiveX, so I haven't a clue how he chose it as a book topic.

However, I can explain the bunny.

As a child, Carlton loved the movie *Harvey* (the film about a man and his six-foot invisible rabbit). The movie so moved Carlton that soon after seeing it, he found his own invisible friend, whom he named Jimmy Stewart.

Carlton and his invisible friend did everything together. They climbed trees, and when Carlton fell and broke his arm, so did his invisible friend. When Carlton skinned his knee, so did his invisible friend. When Carlton caught pneumonia, so did his invisible friend.

Well, it finally turned out that Carlton's invisible friend wasn't invisible after all. In fact, he actually was Jimmy Stewart. The Egremonts immediately kicked him out of the house and he went on to star in many more fine motion pictures.

Carlton never forgot about the talking rabbit, so from my point of view Mr. Bunny is the only thing in this book that makes any sense. But don't take my word for it, I'm just the technical editor.

Oops, you'd better put the book down. I think you've been spotted.

Gary Swanberg
June 1998

Preface

Three major events have changed the way we live as we near the turn of the century, and when we discover what they are, the world will be a better place. Meanwhile, there's ActiveX.

When I first approached myself about writing this book, I was taken aback. After all, what did I know about ActiveX? Sure, it was a computer technology, and I had once seen a computer in a shopping mall. But could ActiveX be covered in a single book? Of course not. Yet on deeper reflection, I concluded, "Why not try? It might be worth a buck." Besides, this topic is too important to leave to the experts.

So in the spring of 1997 I phoned my answering machine from a hotel room in Maui and recorded the outline of the book you now hold. Several calls were necessary, and other messages were received in between. (This explains the lengthy chapter about my Aunt Mable's painful bunions.)

I flew back to the mainland bursting with enthusiasm, but my challenge had just begun. ActiveX is a great topic for a book, but it lacks the entertainment value, say, of a drug-addicted mother having an affair with her teenage daughter's best friend. I needed a gimmick, something to compete with daytime television.

I considered writing the book in a made-up nonsense language, but this had already been done.

I attempted an epic poem, but nothing rhymed with "COMPOBJ.DLL."

I even tried to cast Marlon Brando as ActiveX. He would not return my calls.

In the end, no gimmick seemed right. The technology would just have to speak for itself, and let the chips fall where they may.

So that's the book. Is it just another rehash of the help files already available on your system? You decide. Some readers of an early draft have questioned the talking rabbit angle. What? Isn't every computer book written this way?

CE3
1997

Introduction

A big wet tear plopped from Farmer Jake's cheek.

"Jeepers, Mr. Bunny," he said. "This just ain't my year. I finally got the lower forty plowed, then I find out I need a new kind of fertilizer. And now all this talk of ActiveX has got me confused as an armadillo in a room full of typewriters."

Mr. Bunny knew exactly what the old farmer meant. His long floppy ears twitched as he nibbled thoughtfully on his carrot and considered Farmer Jake's troubles.

Millions of programmers now find themselves in the same predicament as the crusty old farmer. In today's climate of pesticide-free programming languages, high pH acronyms and rapid growth hormone injections, many software engineers are simply mulching their résumés in frustration. If only we could return to those halcyon days when all you had to do was feed the tractor, lube the ox, and code the next generation of Pong in your gazebo by the light of the citronella candle. Well forget it. MS Time Travel version 1.0 has a fatal bug that sends users back to the Pleistocene age due to a 2 digit date error.

So we must look to the future, and Mr. Bunny can help. But before we go hopping down the information bunny trail with Mr. Bunny and Farmer Jake, let's review the rules of the road.

About This Book

Mr. Bunny's Guide to ActiveX is a guide for preschoolers and professional programmers who want to learn everything there is to know about ActiveX. Much of the material presented here is not available elsewhere.

The book contains sample code, the debugging of which is left as an exercise for the reader. Many screen shots are presented for the benefit of programmers who do not own a computer monitor. Standard technical terminology is combined with baby talk and allegorical dream sequences to trigger a subliminal learning response.

"Or," interjected Mr. Bunny, "we might just cruise around and look at some weird stuff."

Oh boy, thought Farmer Jake.

How to Use This Book

Open the book to the first page and begin scanning words from left to right until their meaning is understood. Continue in this manner until the entire page has been scanned, then move on to the next page. NOTE: This may require physically "turning the page" to bring the next page into view.

If you are interrupted or must otherwise put the book down, you should take steps to remember your current position in the text. This can be accomplished in one of several ways:

- Leave the book open. This works best for interruptions shorter than one or two years.
- Insert a bookmark at your current position. Bookmarks are commercially available at most bookstores, or you may fashion your own from a 4' by 8' sheet of marine-grade plywood.
- Fold down a corner of the current page. Not recommended for rare volumes, ancient scrolls, or stone tablets.
- You may wish to simply count the words already read and jot this number in the margin.

When you are finished with the last page of the book, return to the first page and continue reading. This process can be repeated until you get a life.

How This Book Is Organized

- The book begins with Chapter 0 to avoid skewing the index.

- Chapter 1 makes the case for component based software, primarily for legal reasons.
- Chapter 2 discusses the underpinnings of ActiveX and introduces the concept of Mr. Bunny having some helpful little friends.
- Chapter 3 presents the unauthorized tell-all biography of that fickle lady we know as the Windows Registry.
- Chapter 4 introduces Visual Basic version 5, a breakthrough technology that will assure the proliferation of ActiveX controls everywhere. (Even under my bed, thought Farmer Jake.)
- Chapter 5 examines ActiveX controls, whose profound effect on modern programming paradigms can be compared to the impact of the bagel scissors and the propane soap dish.[1]
- Chapter 6 provides the obligatory discussion of the Internet, with a special emphasis on furniture.
- Finally, bunions are caused by the inflammation of the synovial bursa. We'll examine one woman's experience.[2]

Farmer Jake scratched his whiskers with his rake.

Conventions Used in This Book

Sample code is set in a monospace font such as the following:

```
Private Sub Command1_Click()
          MsgBox "Make check payable to Mr. Bunny"
End Sub, "
```

---

1. *Editor's note:* Upon fact checking this book, it was discovered that the propane soap dish does not really exist. CE3 explains:
    "I felt I should inject some levity in this part of the book, so I 'made up' the idea of the propane soap dish. I'm told that a soap dish requires no energy source (other than gravity to hold the soap, and the dish itself, in place). Therefore the effort of attaching a propane tank to a soap dish has no tangible benefit, and in fact incurs the inconvenience of storing a 20-pound LP tank in your sink or shower. (Larger tanks present an even greater difficulty.) I found the whole idea tremendously amusing, and decided that the topic of ActiveX was not so lofty as to be beyond a bit of humor."
    You may laugh now.
2. *Editor's note*: This chapter was deemed too disturbing for young children, and has been removed from the latest edition of the book.

said Mr. Bunny.

The following icons will be used:

 About 15%

 Helpful Hints

 Facilities.

 Circular references.

 Icon-free zone.

" "

Someone is talking.

Examples are set apart in a bold italic font.
Example:
Example:

On each page a value of the form *n* appears, where *n* is a series of one or more digits representing the current page number.

Example:
```
1
```

The familiar dot ' . ' symbol from Internet addresses is used in this book to terminate sentences.

Words in *underlined italics* are hyperlinks. To access these links, carefully remove the mouse cursor from your computer monitor and place it on the page. (You will be unable to use your computer during this time.) Move the cursor with your finger or any other pointing device, then clap your hands to go to the link. If this doesn't work, you may need a *driver upgrade*.

Because today's popular development environments provide code generators able to produce lots of boilerplate code, it is no longer politically correct to refer to programmers as "he or she." Programmers in this book will be referred to as "he, she or it."

A continuation symbol is used when a line is too long to fit within the marg

Finally, at the end of the "Conventions Used in This Book" section, this sentence appears.

Chapter 0

Every adventure must begin somewhere. This one begins on the next page.

The Adventure Begins

Mr. Bunny was still considering Farmer Jake's predicament as the two sat on the farmer's porch. The wise little rabbit adjusted his bifocals and wiggled his pink button nose. "ActiveX is just a new way of controlling your pixels," he said at last. "Can you say 'pixel'?"

The old farmer sure could!

"Pixel," he drawled with ease.

Like Farmer Jake, most computer professionals have heard this technical term[3], but a review of the basics is nonetheless important to: a) establish the groundwork for a firm understanding of ActiveX, and b) increase our page count to meet the expectations of the publisher. So bear with us as Mr. Bunny explains that a pixel is a *picture element*, the smallest part of an image that can be displayed.

"A pixel is a *picture element*, the smallest part of an image that can be displayed," explained Mr. Bunny.

See Figure 1.

"Only by carefully controlling your pixels can you successfully engage today's sophisticated user," said the furry little fellow.

---

3.   And those who have named their cat after it are technically known as *nerds*.

3

Figure 1: Pixel.

"The explosion of the Internet has fueled the need for new buzzwords," continued the rabbit. "OLE, COM, DCOM, MAPI, JMAPI, ISAPI, and MTV have all set the standard for attention spans. Applications have learned how to sing and dance, and the concept of *active content* has empowered the user to interact with their pixels in new and exciting ways."

The cute little cottontail took another bite of his carrot.

"See figures 2 and 3, " he said.

Figure 2: Active Content (Example 1)

Figure 3: Active Content (Example 2)

Mr. Bunny was about to continue when a hollow thud distracted him. It was the sound of Farmer Jake's head hitting the porch rail.

"Zzzzz," went Farmer Jake.

Oh dear, thought Mr. Bunny. ActiveX is going to be harder to explain than I thought.

"Here," said the rabbit, shaking the farmer awake. "Take a bite of my magic cookie, and I'll show you all you need to know."

So Farmer Jake nibbled the cookie, and the world began to change. He was no longer on his back porch!

"Must be goin' through another dang worm hole," thought the farmer, clutching his favorite rake as he and Mr. Bunny were whisked through space and time.

Back to the Garden

Farmer Jake and Mr. Bunny twinkled down in a sparkling landscape of flowers and Tinker Toys. At least that's what it looked like to old Jake. He could still taste the chocolatey goodness of the magic cookie, and wished he had some fresh milk from old Bessie.

"This is our first stop," said Mr. Bunny. "Tell me what you see."

Farmer Jake scratched his head with his garden rake.

"Well, these rods and spools look like them toys I had when I was knee-high to a crustacean," said the farmer. "But they seem to be growin' right before my eyes!"

"That's right," replied Mr. Bunny. "These are OLE interfaces. This is the garden of component-based software!"

As Farmer Jake watched, colorful components queried, interfaced, connected, reference counted, processed, disconnected, reconnected and even preconnected. It was a fascinating ballet, but to the old farmer it all made absolutely no sense whatsoever.

"It doesn't need to make sense," said Mr. Bunny. "It works! And that's the whole point." Sure enough, as Farmer Jake looked closely, he saw text documents turn into dancing teacups. He heard a spreadsheet sing a little song. And everywhere web pages fluttered down like flower petals. It was the spiffiest business

Mr. Bunny's Guide to ActiveX

solution he had ever seen!

"You're right," said Farmer Jake, his spirits lifting at last. "It does seem to work. So this is ActiveX?"

"ActiveX is a collection of technologies that make all this possible," said Mr. Bunny.

Indeed, individuals and corporations alike are demanding that useless white space be eradicated once and for all. As an enabling technology, ActiveX provides the crayons and finger paints to make this possible.

"And now, let's get on with our adventure!" said Mr. Bunny. And with a thump-a-bump of his lucky feet, the rabbit bounded off through the garden of component-based software as old Farmer Jake huffed and puffed to keep up in his big old overalls.

Summary

- There are two main characters in this guide to ActiveX: Farmer Jake and Mr. Bunny.
- Farmer Jake represents the professional software engineer struggling to keep apace with rapidly changing technologies while carrying a garden rake.
- Mr. Bunny represents a talking rabbit.

Exercises

1. Jumping jacks.
2. Push-ups.
3. Deep knee bends.

Additional Reading

- The next chapter.

Just for Fun

Write ActiveX upside down. The answer appears upside down below.

ANSWER: ActiveX

6

Chapter 1

Components change everything. Component-based software has revolutionized programming in the latter half of the second millennium. No longer do we "write some software." Now we "write some components." No longer do we "point and click." Now we "drag and drop." Our stereo systems do not simply consist of components – well actually, they do consist of components.

But is the component revolution beneficial? Or is it just the industry's way of saying, "Throw away all your old software and start over?"?

This chapter examines these issues.

The Case for Component-Based Software

"Components are good," said Mr. Bunny.
Farmer Jake nodded.

NOTES

Chapter 2

As a software developer, it is important to have a mental model of the software components you use. It does not need to be a detailed model – after all, many of us are able to drive a car without understanding the workings of an internal combustion engine. Yet when we look under the hood, we would be very surprised to see a hamster in a wheel or a cook frying spicy Italian sausage.

This chapter looks under the hood of ActiveX. Specifically, the COM architecture is discussed. If you are a Visual Basic programmer, these details are none of your business. Skip to the next chapter.

If you do not care what happens to Mr. Bunny or Farmer Jake, skip the rest of the book.

"This code is probably a nightmare to maintain!"
Matt Pietrek
Windows Internals

The Underpinnings of ActiveX

Mr. Bunny and Farmer Jake came to a clearing in the garden. It was a pleasant plot of grass surrounded by little plastic lawn ornaments. Farmer Jake counted fifteen of the brightly painted gnomes.

The old farmer leaned on his rake as Mr. Bunny began his discussion of ActiveX.

"ActiveX is based on the family of technologies formerly referred to as OLE," began the floppy-eared rabbit.

In fact, ActiveX is just OLE with a different spelling and pronunciation. This was an important change, because everyone felt like an idiot saying 'olé'.

The basic component of ActiveX is the *component*. In mathematics, a component is defined as one of a set of two or more vectors having a sum equal to a given vector. However, we require a more rigorous definition. For our purposes, a component shall be defined as: *a little box with lollipops sticking out*. See Figure 2.1.

Each 'lollipop' in Figure 2.1 represents an interface. The IUnknown interface is shown on top because of its special place in the *Component Object Model* (COM): it is the *all day sucker* of interfaces.

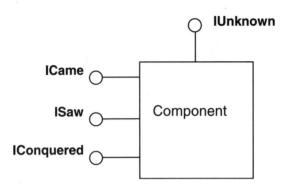

Figure 2.1: Component

"The ActiveX technologies make it possible to dynamically locate and link to interfaces both locally and remotely," said Mr. Bunny. "In other words, components can find each other anywhere in the world, much like bullfrogs croaking in the night."

"It's sort of romantic," murmured Farmer Jake, remembering his younger days and that sweet little girl who lived by the swamp. What was her name? Stinky.

Mr. Bunny continued. "In the old days, calling a function was easy. For example, in the following code fragment:

```
void Foo()
{
    Bar();
}
```

function Foo calls function Bar."

Farmer Jake scratched his head.

"Foo and Bar are the required entry points for sample code," explained Mr. Bunny. "Nobody knows what they mean because the original documentation was fouled up beyond all recognition. And I don't mean fouled."

Farmer Jake understood.

 Do not use *void where prohibited*.

Mr. Bunny went on to explain the evolution of the function call.

"It is possible to take the address of Bar and call it call through a function pointer," he said.

The following code fragment illustrates:

```
(*
```

A slightly larger fragment makes this clearer:

```
(*&Bar)();
```

"This idea can be extended indefinitely," explained the clever bunny rabbit.

```
(*&(*&(*&(*&(*&(*&(*&(*&(*&Bar)))))))))();
```

Mr. Bunny went on to explain how the Windows API formalized this notion with the FARPROC typedef. (A FARPROC is a procedure that is too far away to see.) The GetProcAddress function returns a pointer to such a procedure.

```
Foo = GetProcAddress(hLibrary, "Foo");
```

Earlier versions of Windows required the function pointer to be returned to the library before anyone noticed it missing:

```
ReturnProcAddress(hLibrary, Foo);
```

This and the companion function PayOverdueProcAddressFine became obsolete because they made no sense.

"Then C++ came along with virtual functions," continued Mr. Bunny. "A *virtual function* does not really exist, so there is much less code to write. This is the single biggest reason for the popularity of C++."

Mr. Bunny showed Farmer Jake the following example to illustrate the power of C++.

```
class Doodle {
        virtual void Draw() {};
};
```

"The declaration of the Doodle class contains a virtual Draw method that does nothing," explained the rabbit. Then he derived some useful Doodle classes:

```
class Artist : public Doodle {
     virtual void Draw();
};

class Gunslinger : public Doodle {
     virtual void Draw();
};
```

"These two classes each provide a different implementation of the Draw method," the rabbit explained.

To try Mr. Bunny's example, go buy a C++ compiler, learn how to type, enter the following program, then compile and run it.

```
int main()
{
     Doodle* pArtist = new Artist;
     Doodle* pGunslinger = new Gunslinger;

     pArtist->Draw();
     pGunslinger->Draw();

     delete pArtist;
     delete pGunslinger;
}
```

"The output from this example is a half finished sketch of a gunslinger and a dead artist," said Mr. Bunny.

You may now wish to return the C++ compiler for a full refund.

Vtables

"When you declare a virtual function in C++, the compiler adds the function pointer to a table of virtual functions known as a *Vtable*," said the pink-nosed little bunny.

Poor Farmer Jake seemed confused. He had used C++ – he had even used function pointers – but like many agriculturists, he hadn't thought much about how virtual functions worked.

"Imagine that you and your neighbor each must attend a different function on a certain Saturday evening," said Mr. Bunny. "Let's call this the *Saturday* function."

"Like when I had to judge the Miss County Irrigation Ditch contest on the same night Neighbor Bill celebrated the anniversary of his kidney stone," said Farmer Jake.

Mr. Bunny nodded.

16

"Each of you marks the address of the function on your calendar. When Saturday arrives you each look on your calendar - your *Vtable,*" winked the bunny, "to look up the address of your Saturday function."

But the farmer wasn't paying attention. "The night he passed that stone Neighbor Bill howled so loud he roused half the county," chuckled old Jake. "Poor Bessie nearly kicked down the barn door."

"Let's move on," said Mr. Bunny.

 Take the time to optimize your code. For example, lunch can often be replaced by a table driven dinner.

COM

"Next, let's look at COM," said Mr. Bunny. "The first thing you need to understand about COM is that you do not need to understand COM to use ActiveX."

Farmer Jake did not understand.

"Here are some fun facts," said Mr. Bunny.

- COM stands for *Component Object Model.* Compare this to COM, which stands for *Component Object Model.*
- It is a binary standard, i.e., it is either standard or not.
- Data can be marshaled across the process boundary through a process known as *smuggling.*
- COM should be used only in a well-ventilated area.
- COM objects may live in a DLL, an EXE, or in a rest area in Winnemucca, Nevada.
- COM has been around since 1492, when Christopher Columbus mistook it for India.

"Now," Mr. Bunny continued, "let's sing a little song to help you remember."

Oh boy! thought Farmer Jake.

"We'll sing to the tune of *jingle-bells,*" said the rabbit.

COM COM COM
COM COM COM

COM COM COM COM COM
COM COM COM COM COM COM COM
COM COM COM COM COM COM COM
Hey!
(repeats)

Resolving DLL Based Functions

Now that you are familiar with some of the ways by which a function address can be resolved, let's examine the little ornaments positioned around the garden. These gaily painted lawn gnomes (or *DLLs*) provide a mechanism whereby a code image can be resolved. The DLL mechanism is one of the basic building blocks of your bloated Windows directory. Once grasped, it is not such a great leap to understand COM, OLE, ActiveX, and corporate tax law.

The difference between COM, OLE, and ActiveX

Many people are confused about the difference between COM, OLE, and ActiveX. Let's clear up this confusion once and for all.

COM and OLE both have three letters, whereas ActiveX has seven. COM and OLE share one letter ('O') in common. ActiveX shares the letter 'C' with COM and 'E' with OLE, but it generally does not capitalize them.

As you have already learned, COM is an acronym. OLE was formerly an acronym, but its acronym status has been revoked. ActiveX never stood for anything, but it sounds cooler than the other two acronyms put together (which incidentally spell *comole*, an Italian dish made with mozzarella cheese and wine corks).

The following simple example will show how the DLL mechanism works. Take it away, Mr. B!

Mr. Bunny winked a bunny wink and waved his magic carrot. Why, the whole glen began to shimmer! Little bells tinkled and for a moment the air seemed made of rippled glass.

Suddenly, one of the 15 lawn gnomes popped to life, stepped forward, and bowed.

"Dagnabbit!" cried Farmer Jake. "You just scared the bejeepers out of me."

"Very sorry," said the gnome. "Allow me to introduce myself. I am 96de0250-cbc1-11d0-bb0b-0000c0cf6ecf Smith. But you can call me 96de0250-cbc1-11d0-bb0b-0000c0cf6ecf."

"Smitty is a registered component implemented in a DLL," explained Mr. Bunny. "Don't worry about his funny long name just yet. It has to do with the Windows Registry."

The Windows Registry is discussed in Chapter 3.

"And now it's time for our little demonstration!" Mr. Bunny reached into his magic rucksack and WHOOSH! Out popped Matty the Mat, a big blue floor mat.

"Howdy, Mr. Bunny," said Matty. "What am I today?"

"Today you represent the process space of a running executable," said Mr. Bunny as Matty plopped himself down with a grin.

"Now," said Mr. Bunny to the bewildered farmer, "watch as the following code fragment executes."

```
hLib = LoadLibrary("SMITTY.DLL");
```

As soon as LoadLibrary was called, Smitty tumbled out onto the mat and struck a fine pose. 10 points from the Rumanian judge!

"Very nice," winked Matty.

Smitty smiled, but he required additional DLLs before his entry point could be called. In a flash two more gnomes came to life and tumbled onto the mat. "I'm Chuck!" said Chuck. "I'm Lenny!" said Lenny. And quicker than Farmer Jake could spit a stream of tobacky juice, Smitty hopped up onto Chuck and Lenny's shoulders and clasped their little elfin hands as a series of GetProcAddress calls completed.

Mr. Bunny explained. "The LoadLibrary function brings a DLL image into memory and returns a library handle. The library handle is then passed to the GetProcAddress function, which returns a function pointer. And that's what puts the 'DLL' in DLL!"

But the show was not over!

Lenny and Chuck required DLLs of their own. For a moment the glen was a blur of tumbling gnomes as Chuck loaded Betty and Betty loaded Bing and Bing loaded all those system DLLs with the long white beards. Only when all of the implicitly linked DLLs (gnomes) were loaded and all the procedure addresses (elfin hands) were resolved (clasped) in the process space (Matty) did control (Farmer Jake's attention) finally return to Mr. Bunny.

"And that takes care of the implicit link DLLs," announced the jolly rabbit.

Implicit Link DLLs

As you can see, a lot of work takes place when DLLs are implicitly loaded. But how does the mechanism work? Let's get serious for a moment.

First Windows loads the executable header into memory. The header contains the file name of each required DLL. (The exact structure of the header is beyond the scope of this Mr. Bunny adventure.) You can examine this list yourself with the DUMPBIN.EXE program that ships with Visual C/C++. Just type the following on a command line:

```
dumpbin smitty.dll /imports
```

The output lists all DLLs required by smitty.dll, along with all of the imported procedures it uses. You can use this same command to examine other DLLs by renaming them "smitty.dll."

Once the EXE header is in memory, Windows calls LoadLibrary to load each of the import DLLs listed there, and uses GetProcAddress to resolve the procedure addresses. This process repeats recursively as each DLL is loaded, and concludes when all the little gnomes have tumbled out onto Matty the Mat.

Farmer Jake blinked at a teetering tottering pyramid of lawn gnomes. Smitty stood on Lenny and Chuck, and Lenny and Chuck stood on Betty and Bing and Wally and Willy, and Betty and Bing and Wally and Willy stood on Msvcrt40.Dll and Msvcirt.Dll and Msvcrt.dll and GDI.Dll and Kernal.Dll and Advapi32.Dll and User32.Dll and Comdlg32.Dll.[4]

All fifteen gnomes had come to life!

"Now things get interesting," said Mr. Bunny. "COM has taught these old gnomes some spiffy new tricks."

Using COM

The LoadLibrary mechanism is fine for locating C style functions, but what about C++ methods? What if the users of a DLL don't want to use C++? What if they don't like it? What if they have a secret grudge because C+ tricked their ex-fiancés into marrying someone else even though the baby wasn't really theirs? Clearly an object's interface should not play favorites. It must be accessible

---

4.   This example has been somewhat oversimplified. Actual system DLL dependencies create a lopsided pyramid that would have fallen over before Mr. Bunny made his next point.

from any programming language[5].

Dynamically loading a C++ method from a DLL presents two major difficulties.

First, C++ mangles the function names. Some compilers refer to this as "decoration." For example, a C++ compiler might take this simple function:

```
int f();
```

and decorate it like this:

```
           f
          @@
         @_@
        @_@@_@
       @_@?KG_@
      @UA@_AF_@
     @_U@E@A@I@Z_@
          ||
       MBEUAFX
```

Secondly, C++ methods require an object pointer. Where are you going to get one of those at 11 o'clock on a Saturday night? The helper functions found in COMPOBJ.DLL can help. Just keep your eye on Smitty as he reverses his jacket.

Drum roll please…

Oh boy! Smitty is a circus ringmaster!

"Watch carefully," said Mr. Bunny.

The glen echoed with the sound of a drum roll as Smitty produced a cell phone and called the following function:

```
STDAPI CoCreateInstance(
    REFCLSID rclsid,          // Big long funny looking identifier
    LPUNKNOWN pUnkOuter,      // Outer unknown, if known
    DWORD dwClsContext,       // Some number
    REFIID riid,              // Another big long funny looking identifier
    LPVOID * ppv              // Pointer to pointer variable storage for
                              // storage of pointer
);
```

Let's look at each parameter while Smitty dials his phone.

The *rclsid* provides the area code, phone, extension, zip code, social security number, age, annual salary, odometer reading and hat size of the component you wish to talk to. Because this identifier is very long, a convenient variable

---

5.   Except COBOL.

should be defined to hold it, as shown below.

```
CLSID d72e8710-9cce_11d0_bad2_0000c0cf6ecf;
```

The *pUnkOuter* parameter points to the outer unknown, if any. The "k" is silent, so "punk" is usually pronounced "pun."

The *dwClsContext* parameter defines the request context for the server housing. It may be any combination of the following:

```
CLSCTX_INPROC_SERVER     = 1
CLSCTX_INPROC_HANDLER    = 2
CLSCTX_LOCAL_SERVER      = 4
CLSCTX_LOCAL_MAITRE_D    = 8
CLSCTX_HOUSE_DRESSING    = a zesty lemon vinaigrette
CLSCTX_DESSERT           = 3.141592
```

You may define as many additional options as you like as long as you do not use them.

The next parameter, *riid*, comes next.

Finally, *ppv* comes last.

Now that you have mastered the CoCreateInstance function, you can see how simple it is to call:

```
// Call the CoCreateInstance function:
 .
 .
 .
...details omitted for clarity...
 .
 .
 .
// ppv now contains an interface pointer
```

Rinnngggggg.

"The call is going through," said Smitty from atop his perch.

"Smitty is contacting an in-process server," said Mr. Bunny. "His call will retrieve an IUnknown interface pointer. He will then be able to use QueryInterface to access the public functionality of the server."

"Darn," said Smitty. "I'm in voice mail."

"Once an IUnknown interface is retrieved, you have the ability to query for other interfaces," explained Mr. Bunny.

"What about inheritance?" asked Farmer Jake.

"QueryInterface is superior to inheritance," explained Mr. Bunny. "With inheritance, you have to wait for someone to die."

"I'm querying for the IFlyingEnchilada interface," said Smitty as he pushed more buttons on the phone.

Farmer Jake and Mr. Bunny waited.

Smitty pushed more buttons.

Farmer Jake picked his teeth with his garden rake.

And waited.

The drum roll continued.

"ActiveX can sure take a long time to get going," said the farmer.

"Software should always be designed for the hardware of the future," said Mr. Bunny. "This works out well, because by the time your application is fully loaded, faster hardware is available and your old computer is obsolete."

Smitty pushed one more button. And suddenly…

TA DA!

The famous high flying IFlyingEnchilada trapeze artists tumbled in from every direction.

The little clearing turned into a big top circus!

A flying trapeze nearly hit Farmer Jake in the head as the Enchiladas took to the sky. And they were working without a net!

Smitty invoked more interfaces, and circus gnomes bounced in from every direction. They flipped in midair and set fire to their hair. The little gnomes were everywhere! On elephant, horse and pig and gnu, they marshaled their data and passed it right through.

Now *this* is active content, thought Farmer Jake as the little gnomes danced all around.

Then suddenly…

BRRR_RUMBLE!!!!

…the earth began to shake.

"It's the Big One!" cried Farmer Jake.

"We must get out of here," said Mr. Bunny. "We're not properly registered – we'll need to jump through some hoops to get our papers."

Smitty the Ringmaster held up a dazzling hoop of fire, and Mr. Bunny and Farmer Jake dove through.

And disappeared!

Summary

- In this chapter we learned basically nothing.
- We have seen that GetProcAddress returns a FARPROC pointer to a named function, if it exists. If GetProcAddress doesn't exist, then why are you using it?
- Farmer Jake and Mr. Bunny have disappeared through a ring of fire.

Exercises

1. Count the lawn ornaments in your neighborhood. How many support the IUnknown interface?
2. Connect the dots:

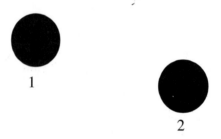

1

2

Additional Reading

- *Inside OLE 2.* Kraig Brockschmidt.
- *United States Internal Revenue Code (Title 26).* Various authors.
- *ActiveX for Bunnies.* Peter Kerplotnik.

Chapter 3

Sooner or later everything turns up in the Windows Registry. Canceled TV shows go there to sulk. Old generals go there to fade away. And those socks that disappear from your rinse cycle? You get the idea.

But what do unfunny sitcoms, military has-beens and missing argyles have to do with ActiveX? Not much, as it turns out.

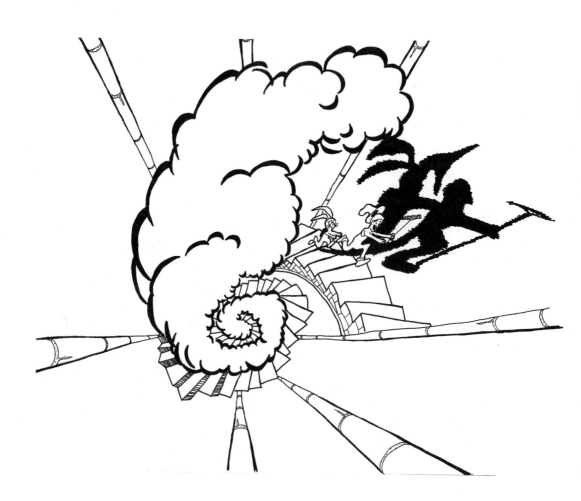

Inside the Registry

"Where are we?" Farmer Jake's voice echoed in the darkness.

Mr. Bunny reached into his rucksack and pulled out a flashlight.

Click!

Farmer Jake blinked in the flashlight beam. They were at the bottom of a long, winding staircase, the kind usually found in a standard file dialog. (See Figure 3.1.)

"This is the Windows Registry," said Mr. Bunny. "From the look of things, it's the HKEY_LOCAL_MACHINE branch. HKEY_LOCAL_MACHINE \SYSTEM\CurrentControlSet\Control\SessionManager\Environment, to be precise."

Sure enough, Mr. Bunny's flashlight played across row on row of environment variables, the very same environment variables Farmer Jake was used to seeing on the Environment tab of the System Properties Control Panel.

"Look, there's the Path," said Farmer Jake.

"Be careful!" cried Mr. Bunny.

But it was too late. With a crash and a clatter, Farmer Jake had knocked several directories loose from the Path environment variable.

Poor Farmer Jake! He tried his best to pick up the pieces. But his rake swung up as he stooped down and with a smash and a shatter, the DOS ComSpec lay in bits, all jumbled up with the remnants of the Path.

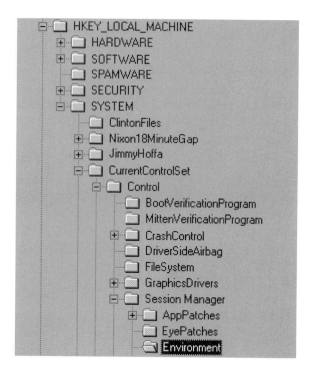

Figure 3.1: A Long Staircase

"Oh dear," said Mr. Bunny. "We'd better get out of here before we do any more damage."

So the pair of adventurers headed for the stairs.

Up they climbed, sneaking past the Session Manager asleep at his desk and the Graphics Drivers delivering fresh fruit and bitmaps.

Finally they reached the FileSystem key, and there they stopped to rest.

 It's a good idea to familiarize yourself with the Windows Registry in case it becomes corrupted. The advanced programmer periodically deletes the Registry and retypes it from memory.

Overview of the Windows Registry

Mr. Bunny and Farmer Jake sat down to rest against the FileSystem key. Mr. Bunny turned off the flashlight and spoke quietly in the dark.

"Every day millions of disk sectors go unused," he said. "The Windows Registry helps solve this problem by accumulating information about every device you ever attach to your computer and every version of all the software you ever try."

The crusty old cropper scratched his head. "I get it! It's like a directory structure, a hierarchical database in which directory names correspond to record keys," he drawled.

"You could say that, but I look at it this way: Remember the time we reorganized your compost heap?"

How could Farmer Jake forget? It was the best day of his life!

"We put the orange peels on the left," said Mr. Bunny. "And the lawn clippings on the right. And Bessie's cow pies went right up on top."

Mmmm, thought Farmer Jake. The tomatoes *were* delicious that year.

"Well the Registry does for Windows what we did for your compost heap. The old AUTOEXEC.BAT, CONFIG.SYS, SYSTEM.INI, WIN.INI, and every WHATEVER.INI from every vendor in the world can now go away. They have all been neatly filed in the Windows Registry, just like your lawn clippings and other organic refuse."

Planned Obsolescence

The files mentioned by Mr. Bunny can still be found on many systems. For example, certain settings in the AUTOEXEC.BAT file are honored when your 32-bit system starts up. Specifically, path settings and environment variable specifications will take effect when the system starts. Also, the handling of batch file REM statements is not expected to change in the near future.

As for all those INI files, it will take a long time before they completely disappear, but Microsoft is providing a clear path to their obsolescence. Specifically, the familiar *PrivateProfile* function family now supports "write-through" to the Windows Registry, but only on some systems. Write-through is not supported under Windows 95, and the functions are not available at all on the earlier ENIAC system.

Lastly, if you use Visual Basic, the *SaveSettings* and *GetSettings* subroutines write directly to the Windows Registry. In fact, you must make a special effort to import the old profile string API if you want to use INI files.

With an installed base of well over a dozen users, Microsoft must move slowly when migrating to new technologies.

Something scurried past Farmer Jake's feet.
Mice!

Registering Class Identifiers

"Dagblam!" cried Farmer. "If there's one thing I can't stand, it's mice!" He jumped to his feet in the darkness. He could hear the sound of little trackballs rolling across the floor.

"Well, let's be moving on then," said Mr. Bunny. "If we can find the class identifiers, we'll be able to get our papers in order."

But things were not going to be so easy.

Click click click.

Oh my! The flashlight would not turn on. The battery was dead!

"Here," said Farmer Jake. "I have a match."

"NO!" cried Mr. Bunny.

But the old geezer was just too fast. WHOOSH! The FileSystem key went up in flames!

"Let's MOVE!" cried Mr. Bunny, and the pair ran for the stairs amid the WHOOP WHOOP WHOOP of smoke alarms.

Up up up they climbed, smoke billowing behind them.

 Do not use matches near the Windows Registry.

"Shhh," said Mr. Bunny as the pair rounded a corner. "Security is on this level." But no sooner had he spoken than lights flashed and sirens screamed and security guards scampered everywhere!

"Quick, this way!" Mr. Bunny grabbed Farmer Jake and the two adventurers ducked behind a door labeled Software as a fire truck whizzed past.

"Now try not to touch anything," whispered Mr. Bunny.

The door closed behind them and once again they were in darkness. But that clever Mr. Bunny was always prepared! He rummaged in his rucksack and came up with his trusty night vision goggles. In a moment he was leading Farmer Jake down a flight of stairs to the CLSID branch.

"Here we go," said Mr. Bunny at last. "I've found the lights."

And in a snap, the room was brightly lit. From floor to ceiling, all Farmer Jake could see were funny numbers, just like Smitty's first name. See Figure 3.2.

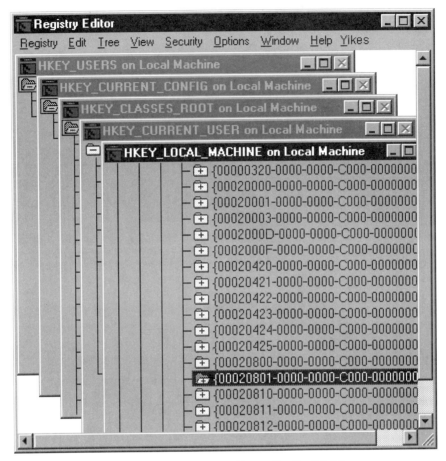

Figure 3.2: Mr. Bunny Turns On the Lights

"Will you lookee there," said Farmer Jake. "I see my missing insurance forms!"

Mr. Bunny returned the night goggles to his rucksack, and pulled out Lenny the Laptop!

"Good morning, Mr. Bunny," beeped Lenny.

"We need to get ourselves some class identifiers," said Mr. Bunny. "The following command ought to do the trick."

Tappety-tappety-tap, Mr. Bunny typed the following command on Lenny's keypad.

```
uuidgen -n2
```

"I feel all tingly," twittered Lenny as the following class identifiers were generated.

```
16014620-d12e-11d0-bb13-0000c0cf6ecf
16014621-d12e-11d0-bb13-0000c0cf6ecf
```

"Take your pick," said Mr. Bunny. "Both identifiers are unique in all the world."

"How can you be sure?" asked Farmer Jake.

"I checked," winked the clever rabbit. Farmer Jake picked the first number because somehow it looked more unique. Then Mr. Bunny quickly typed the following into a text file:

```
HKEY_CLASSES_ROOT\CLSID\{16014620-d12e-11d0-bb13-
0000c0cf6ecf} = Farmer Jake
HKEY_CLASSES_ROOT\CLSID\{16014620-d12e-11d0-bb13-
0000c0cf6ecf}\ProgID = Farmer.Jake
HKEY_CLASSES_ROOT\CLSID\{16014620-d12e-11d0-bb13-
0000c0cf6ecf}\InProcServer32 = C:\win-
dows\system32\FarmerJ.ocx
HKEY_CLASSES_ROOT\CLSID\{16014621-d12e-11d0-bb13-
0000c0cf6ecf } = Mr. Bunny
HKEY_CLASSES_ROOT\CLSID\{16014621-d12e-11d0-bb13-
0000c0cf6ecf}\ProgID = Mr.Bunny
HKEY_CLASSES_ROOT\CLSID\{16014621-d12e-11d0-bb13-
0000c0cf6ecf}\InProcServer32 = C:\win-
dows\system32\MrBunny.ocx[6]
```

"The Windows Registry is a great improvement over the INI files it replaces," explained Mr. Bunny as he finished typing. "Unlike INI files, the Windows Registry cannot be inadvertently changed with a text editor. You must use the Registry Editor to make inadvertent changes."

And so Mr. Bunny selected the Import Registry File command from the Registry Editor's File menu and imported his homemade text file.

"Weee, that tickles," giggled the farmer as he and Mr. Bunny were immortalized in the Windows Registry.

---

6.   Contrary to popular belief, CLSID registry entries, when spelled backwards, do not contain the subliminal message "I worship Satan."

Summary

- The Windows Registry contains all of your hardware, software, and operating system configuration information, plus peanuts and a prize.
- You can use REGEDIT.EXE or REGEDT32.EXE to corrupt the Windows Registry as needed.
- If you damage the Windows Registry, you'll need to buy a new computer.

Exercises

1. Write a hierarchical database system.
2. Help Farmer Jake find his favorite rake.

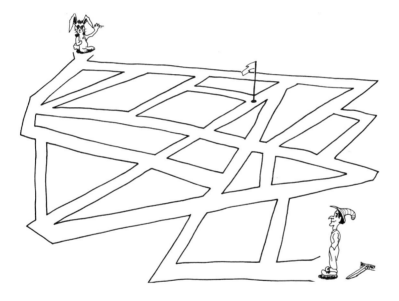

Additional Reading

- *New York City Phone Book.*
- *Hong Kong Yellow Pages.*
- *Barney's Big Book of System Administration.* Abdul O'Malley.

Chapter 4

See Visual Basic. See Visual Basic run.

"There was a smell in the house;
it had always been there."
William Gibson
Mona Lisa Overdrive

Visual Basics

In this chapter you will learn:

- How to install Visual Basic
- How to run Visual Basic
- How to create a Visual Basic form
- How to add controls to your Visual Basic form
- How to crash Visual Basic and lose all of your work
- What Mr. Bunny and Farmer Jake do next

A light lunch will be served.

What Is Visual Basic?

Visual Basic is the Windows development environment that says to C and C++ programmers: "What makes you think you're so special?" It is based on the earlier VISUAL programming language, a language consisting solely of the GOTO statement and lots of frantic waving.

Here are just a few of the things you can do with Visual Basic:

- Start it up
- Look at all the menu items
- Move the toolbars around
- Maximize the application
- Quit

Installation

Visual Basic can be installed by running the Setup program, or you may use this easy shortcut.

You will need:

- A box of Visual Basic
- A Phillips head screwdriver
- A hammer
- A computer of some sort

Step 1: Pry off the computer's case with the claw end of the hammer. The inside of the computer will appear.

Step 2: Gently position the screwdriver against the top of the hard drive.

Step 3: Rap sharply on the screwdriver with the hammer until you've made a small hole in the drive housing. Be careful not to damage the screwdriver.

Step 4: Pour in the contents of your Visual Basic box. Try not to spill anything.

Step 5 (optional): Add help files, sample code and seasonings.

Step 6: Reseal the hole with wood putty or quick setting concrete.

Step 7: Put your computer back together. If your system supports plug-and-play, you can discard any leftover parts.

Visual Basic is now ready to use. What are you waiting for? Start it up!

Running Visual Basic

To run Visual Basic, you must first figure out where it is. Select the "Find Files or Folders" command from your Start menu, as shown in Figure 4.1.

Figure 4.1: Finding Stuff

 You may first need to run the Find Computer command if you have misplaced your PC.

When the following dialog appears, enter *.* in the field named *Named*.

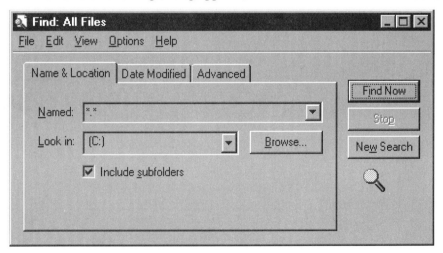

Figure 4.1.1: Searching for Visual Basic

Now click Find Now. The Find command will present you with a list of all your files. Search through these files until you see something that looks like

Visual Basic, then double-click it. Alternately, you may double-click on everything until Visual Basic appears to be running.

If the Find command is unable to display all of your files, then you should narrow the search by deleting files from your hard drive until the entire list can be displayed. If after deleting all of your files you are still unable to run Visual Basic, call Microsoft Technical Support.

When Visual Basic is launched, a splash screen appears. The Visual Basic 5.0 splash screen is shown in Figure 4.1.1.1.

Figure 4.1.1.1: Visual Basic 5.0 splash screen

Creating a Form

In Visual Basic, you form windows using *forms*. A *form* is a window that you form. At first forms are unformed. You must form your forms using the form designer (formerly the *former*). In the form former, an unformed form forms a uniform formation of dots, as shown in Figure 4.1.1.1.1.

Make a quick count of the dots. You will be held responsible for any that you lose.

Figure 4.1.1.1.1: Form (Top View)

Figure 4.1.1.1.1.1: Form (Side View)

When you first run Visual Basic, a default form called Form1 is created. If you do not like this name, then select the Add Form command from the Project menu. A dialog similar to Figure 4.1.1.1.1.1.1 appears.

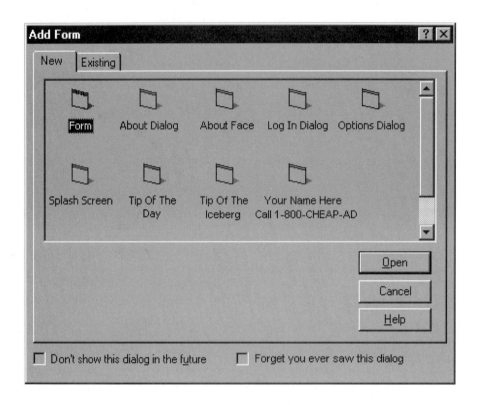

Figure 4.1.1.1.1.1.1: Add Form Dialog

Highlight the Form icon. (It's the icon that looks like all the other icons.) Click Open to create the new form. The new form will be called Form2. Continue to add forms until a form is created with a name that you like. Then delete the unused forms.

The Toolbox

Before you add a control to your form, you must add it to the Visual Basic toolbox. The Visual Basic toolbox is like a real toolbox except a real toolbox holds actual tools. Compare this to Farmer Jake's toolbox, which occasionally holds a liverwurst sandwich.

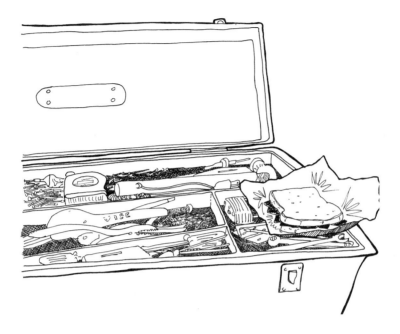

Figure 4.1.1.1.1.1.1.1: Farmer Jake's Toolbox

The Visual Basic toolbox holds *controls*. When you first start Visual Basic, a standard set of controls is available, as shown in table 1.

Table 1   Toolbar Icons

Icon	Description
↖	This is the only pointer in Visual Basic. (Objects in Visual Basic are passed by rumor and innuendo, never by pointer.) Be careful, you'll poke your eye out.
	The Picture control shows the view from Farmer Jake's back porch during last year's drought.
A	Letter 'A' control. Third party vendors are expected to provide controls for the rest of the alphabet.

The TextBox control allows you to get input from the user. You should normally ignore the input and do things your own way.

The Moat control keeps the pagan masses away from your castle.

CommandButton control. Simple and understated, yet pouty and provocative.

Use the CheckBox control to store canceled checks.

Cyclops control. Keep the pointer away from this one.

The ListBox control allows the user to select an item from a list, in accordance with ancient cabalistic ritual.

A coin-operated ListBox.

HScrollBar control. Scrolls east to west in the northern hemisphere, west to east in the southern hemisphere.

"Golly," says Farmer Jake. "That looks like the town grain elevator."

The Timer control allows your program to crash at predefined intervals.

The SuggestionBox control allows the user to recommend improvements to your application.

The Folder control stores your permanent record since grammar school. Play nice, boys and girls.

Grocery list control.

The Shape control lets you create shapes such as a circle, a square, or a four-dimensional hyper-cube that punctures the fabric of space-time, allowing Zemo of Zolto to lead his invading horde to the pitiful Earthling home world. Ovals and rounded rectangles may also be created.

Image control. Acrylic on canvas.

Stick control. Carrot control must be purchased separately.

The Data control serves as a brain implant, allowing Zemo to remotely stimulate the cerebral cortex of unsuspecting Earthlings.

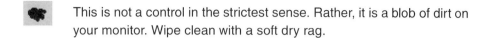 Creates an 'ole in your application to let in other objects.

This is not a control in the strictest sense. Rather, it is a blob of dirt on your monitor. Wipe clean with a soft dry rag.

Let's add some new controls to our toolbox. Select the Components command from the Project menu. When the Components dialog appears, select the components shown in Figure 4.1.1.1.1.1.1.1.1.1.

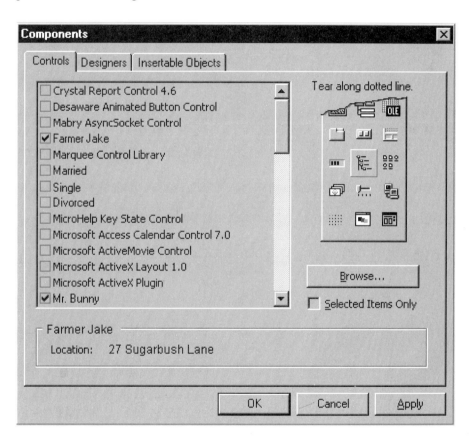

Figure 4.1.1.1.1.1.1.1.1.1: Selecting Controls

Click OK, and the Mr. Bunny and Farmer Jake icons will appear in your toolbox. Your toolbox should look something like Figure 4.1.1.1.1.1.1.1.1.1. (If not, you have done something terribly wrong.)

Figure 4.1.1.1.1.1.1.1.1.1:
Mr. Bunny and Farmer Jake appear in your toolbox.

Now you are ready to add the new controls to your form. Click on the Mr. Bunny icon, then click on your form and drag out a small furry rectangle.

Look! It's Mr. Bunny!

Now do the same for that funny old Farmer Jake.

Isn't programming fun!

Down on the Form

POOF!

"What happened?" said Farmer Jake.

Old Jake and Mr. Bunny stood on a vast landscape dotted with strange dark holes.

"It appears we have been instantiated in the Visual Basic form designer," replied Mr. Bunny, sniffing at one of the holes. He peered over the edge, but the hole was too deep and dark. Nothing could be seen.

"With Visual Basic, a lone novice can accidentally create applications more sophisticated than those created by a highly paid team of software engineers," explained the fluffy cottontail. "In fact, Visual Basic *forces* you to create applications by accident."

The curious rabbit hopped over to another mysterious hole and took some readings with a Geiger counter from his trusty rucksack. "This is very odd," he said. "These readings are above normal, even for Visual Basic version 5.0."

The advanced programmer wears a lead suit when working with Visual Basic.

Just then a shadow passed overhead.

"Look!" cried Mr. Bunny. "This is what you've been waiting for. It's an ActiveX control!"

The shadow quickly passed by to the north, and with a loud PLOP a CommandButton dropped to the ground a few hundred twips away.

"Let's go have a look."

"But it looks like such a long walk," said Farmer Jake.

But of course that clever fellow knew a shortcut!

"Here, let me have your property sheet," he said.

"My what?" asked the puzzled farmer.

"At the end of your rake," said Mr. Bunny.

Sure enough, a piece of paper was stuck on the prongs of Farmer Jake's rake. Farmer Jake glanced at the property sheet, and handed it to Mr. Bunny.

Figure 4.1.1.1.1.1.1.1.1.1.1.1: Farmer Jake's Property Sheet

Mr. Bunny took a pencil from his pocket protector and scribbled something on the paper.

FOOP!

Farmer Jake suddenly stood next the CommandButton that a moment ago seemed so far away.

FOOP!

Just like that, Mr. Bunny appeared next to him.

Farmer Jake was amazed, but Mr. Bunny had simply changed the Left and Top properties on their property sheets.

"I simply changed the Left and Top properties on our property sheets," said Mr. Bunny. See Figure 4.1.1.1.1.1.1.1.1.1.1.

You can do the same with a black grease pen. To be sure you can undo your changes, test the grease pen on an unused part of your screen.

Properties

One of the properties of ActiveX controls is that they have properties. If you are a C++ programmer, think of properties as public member variables and access methods of a class. If you are a real estate agent, think of properties as public member variables and access methods of a breakfast nook.

"Even a simple command button has lots of properties," explained Mr. Bunny. He opened a closet door located on the side of the CommandButton.

"These properties control the appearance of the button," said Mr. Bunny.

Farmer Jake looked over everything in the closet, and finally selected a raccoon hat, a necktie made of bacon, and a peach fuzz sport coat.

Other common properties are listed in Table 4 1/10.

Table 4 1/10	Common Properties for ActiveX Controls
Property	*Description*
Channels	Number of cable channels received by the control.
Depth	Maximum depth at the deep end of a splash screen.
Height	Height of the control, in its bare feet.
Left	Determines if the control has gone home early.
Preference	Indicates that the control prefers to sit in the non-smoking section of the form.
PropertyBag	An enumerated type specifying "Paper," "Plastic," or "No Thanks I'll Eat It Here."

SQL	Specifies whether the control is a sequel to an earlier more popular control.
Squid	Provides compatibility with the advanced features expected in future operating systems.
Tag	Contains detailed washing instructions.
Time	Recommended cooking time. Ovens may vary.
Trance	Returns True if the control is channeling the spirit voice of "The Skipper" from *Gilligan's Island*.
Warranty	Normally 5 years or 50,000 mouse clicks.
ZodiacSign	Determines compatibility with other controls.

"We're in luck!" said Mr. Bunny, pointing to an arrow that hovered above them. "The mouse pointer is in easy reach. We should be able to create some more controls."

Your First Visual Basic Application

Mr. Bunny reached into his rucksack and pulled out Sammy the Slingshot. "Find me some rocks," said the rabbit to Farmer Jake. "Let's see if we can hit the toolbox from here."

Farmer Jake raked up a small pile of rocks, and Mr. Bunny loaded one into the slingshot.

"Yummy," said Sammy.

With a snap of his bunny wrist, Mr. Bunny bounced the rock off a control icon in the toolbox.

PING!

Overhead, the cursor changed to a little airplane. (Figure 4.1.1.1.1.1.1.1.1.1.1.1.)

Figure 4.1.1.1.1.1.1.1.1.1.1.1.1: The Airplane Cursor

Then Mr. Bunny reached into his rucksack one more time. YIPPEE-I-O! Out popped Larry Lariat!

"Hi, y'all," drawled Larry.

"Go get 'em," cried Mr. Bunny, and Larry twirled into the sky and lassoed the little airplane.

"Hang on to my tail," shouted Larry.

Mr. Bunny pulled on Larry's tail as the airplane tried to get away. The airplane flew one way and Mr. Bunny pulled the other way, and Larry stretched and stretched, forming a selection rectangle on the form (Figure 4.1.1.1.1.1.1.1.1.1.1.1.1.1).

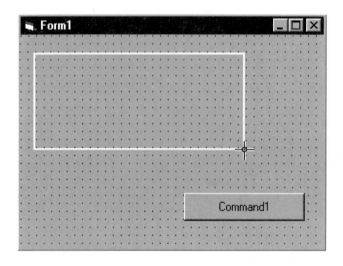

Figure 4.1.1.1.1.1.1.1.1.1.1.1.1.1: Larry the Lariat lassoes an airplane

When Larry thought he could stretch no more, Mr. Bunny decided the new control was just the size he wanted and let go of Larry's tail.

FWIPP!

A brand new control appeared!

"Text1," said the control.

"It's a TextBox control," declared Mr. Bunny.

"Weee, that was fun!" said Larry.

"Can I try?" asked Farmer Jake.

Mr. Bunny handed the slingshot to Farmer Jake.

ZING!

The old Farmer scored a hit on the first try! Larry twirled into the sky once more, and in a wink they had added a vertical scrollbar to the form.

"See how easy Visual Basic is?" said Mr. Bunny.

NOTE

The first scrollbar ever built took 15 months, required 96 megabytes of RAM, and had a weight capacity of only 7 ounces.

Farmer Jake felt like a kid again. "Can I try another?" Mr. Bunny nodded, and the old geezer squealed with delight.

And so Farmer Jake and Mr. Bunny took turns bouncing rocks off the toolbox while Larry lassoed the airplane. And when finally they were done, they had created their first fully functional Visual Basic application (Figure 4.1.1.1.1.1.1.1.1.1.1.1.1.1.1).

And so can you! Just gather up some rocks and sling them at the Visual Basic toolbar. This is especially therapeutic after Visual Basic has crashed for the eleventh time in a day.

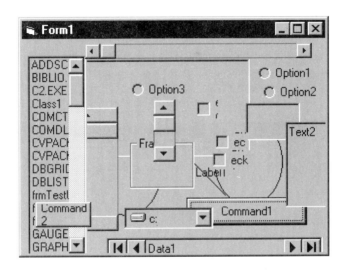

Figure 4.1.1.1.1.1.1.1.1.1.1.1.1.1.1: Your first Visual Basic application

The Toolbar

"Let's try the Visual Basic toolbar," said Mr. Bunny. "If we can hit the ▶ button, we'll bring the application to life."

"What's does '▶' mean?" asked Farmer Jake.

"It's an icon," explained Mr. Bunny. "Icons are an efficient way to communicate a lot of information. Icons will soon allow our written language to merge with the ideograms of China and Japan."

"✄ it out," said Farmer Jake. "You must be making one of your bunny jokes."

But Mr. Bunny was serious, and to **↖?** Farmer Jake understand, he took his high powered 🔭 from his rucksack and gave Farmer Jake a close look at the Visual Basic toolbar far to the north.

"The Visual Basic toolbar is just like a real toolbar, except there is no such thing as a real toolbar," explained Mr. Bunny.

Table 4 2/10 shows the icons Farmer Jake saw through the binoculars.

Table 4 2/10   Toolbar Icons

Icon	Description
	Slice of birthday cake
	Guillotine blade falling into a swimming pool
	Captain Hook's good hand
	Captain Hook's other hand
	Gas pump
	Shark infested waters
	Toaster (top view)
	Mouse pad
	Pandora's box
	Pandora's Tupperware
	Rejected Communist Party symbol
	Bathroom scale
	Mr. Bunny's bifocals
	Patent drawing for a diesel hair brush

Then Mr. Bunny took Petey the Peashooter from his rucksack. Aiming carefully, he bounced a pea off hit the ▶ button.

DING!

The button turned gray.

BRRR_RUMBLE!!!

The earth began to shake!

"Oh no," cried Farmer Jake. "It's another quake!"

"Not quite," said Mr. Bunny, watching closely as camouflage covers slid over the strange holes that dotted the landscape. "Not quite…"

And in a flash Mr. Bunny grabbed Larry and lassoed Farmer Jake and dove into one of the holes.

The lid rumbled and rolled shut above them.

They were falling!

Summary

In this chapter you ~~will~~ learn*ed*:

- How to install Visual Basic
- How to run Visual Basic
- How to create a Visual Basic form
- How to add controls to your Visual Basic form
- How to crash Visual Basic and lose all of your work
- What Mr. Bunny and Farmer Jake ~~do~~ next

did

Exercises

1. Point
2. Click
3. Find the missing poodle

Additional Reading

- *The Velveteen Rabbit.* Margery Williams.
- *Incompleteness, Nonlocality, and Realism: A Prolegomenon to the Philosophy of Quantum Mechanics for Dummies.* Mitchell Bedhead.
- *Barney's Big Book of Medical Oddities.* Rusty Chen.

Chapter 5

Creating ActiveX controls used to be the domain of C++ gurus. Miscalculate a trajectory, and your whole system went down in flames. Make the wrong incision, and you've lobotomized your career. Rocket scientists and brain surgeons alike were heard to say "At least it's not ActiveX programming."

Visual Basic 5.0 changes all that. With version 5.0, you can easily perform brain surgery on a rocket scientist right in the comfort of your own living room. And while you're at it, you can create some nifty controls!

"Nyuck nyuck nyuck."
Curly
Stooge

ActiveX Controls

Some have likened ActiveX controls to little elves (*ActiveX for Dummies*). Others have compared them to fairy wood nymphs (*ActiveX for Insufferable Dopes*), magical sprites (*ActiveX for Big Stupid Idiots*), and enchanted flying pixies from beyond the Oort cloud (*ActiveX for Insurance Salesmen*).

As professional programmers, we often need such fanciful metaphors to bring us a smile as we merrily traipse through the torturous hell of our existence. But Farmer Jake and Mr. Bunny were about to discover the shocking truth.

Creating an ActiveX Control Project

First, let's create our own ActiveX control. Run Visual Basic 5.0 and select the New Project command from the File menu. The New Project dialog appears, as shown in Figure ⊞.l.

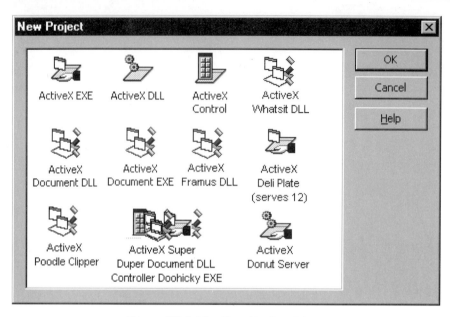

Figure ₩.I: The New Project Dialog

Don't let the bewildering array of ActiveX project choices scare you; this is simply a security feature. Click on the ActiveX Control icon, then click OK. (Or you may place the mouse under your chin, press the TAB and arrow keys with your toes until the ActiveX Control icon is highlighted, then reach behind your head with your right hand and tap yourself on the left shoulder so that, startled, your jaw snaps open and clicks the left mouse button.)

Visual Basic creates a UserControl form. Figure ₩.II shows the top portion of the form.

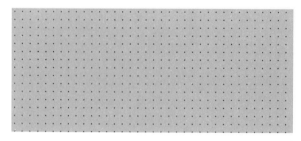

Figure ₩.II: UserControl Form (top portion)

The bottom portion of the form is shown in Figure ‖‖.‖‖.

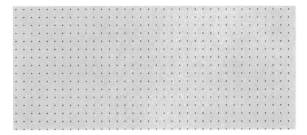

Figure ‖‖.‖‖: UserControl Form (bottom portion)

Next, double-click inside the UserControl form to bring up the Code Window. (This is known as "bringing your form up to code.") The code window for a new User Control is shown in Figure ‖‖.‖‖‖.

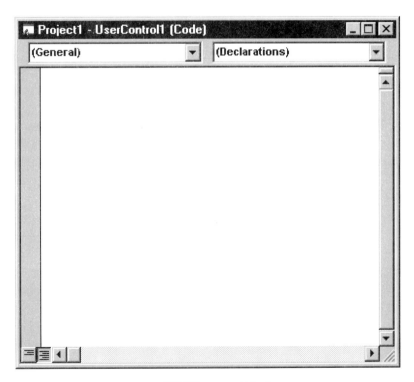

Figure ‖‖.‖‖‖: Code Window

Often this is all the code you'll need.

Finally, scroll the code window until Mr. Bunny and Farmer Jake come into view.

Weeeee!

Mr. Bunny and Farmer Jake were falling through a maze of pipes and ducts and Gantt charts into a vast underground cavern.
"What are we going to do now?" cried the Farmer.
"Hang on!" shouted Mr. Bunny.
He pulled a ripcord on his rucksack.
FLURP!
Out fluffed Petey Parachute!
"Hang on, everyone!" called Petey.
Petey held on to Mr. Bunny and Mr. Bunny held on to Larry and Larry held on to Farmer Jake and they all floated gently to the floor of the cavern.
And Mr. Bunny's suspicions were confirmed.

We'll examine Mr. Bunny's discovery more closely in a moment. First, let's pretend this is a technical book by covering two important attributes of all ActiveX controls: Methods and Events.

Methods

Let's look at a simple method, the Move method common to most controls. We all want to write clean code, and a good way to accomplish this is to periodically sweep up under your controls. The following code moves your control out of the way.

```
' Move the control out of the way
Control1.Move Control1.Left + 20, Control1.Right + 20

' TODO: Add your sweeper code here

' Move the control back
Control1.Move Control1.Left - 20, Control1.Right - 20
```

A broom and dustpan may be sufficient, but for larger projects an industrial vacuum is recommended.

Events

Events occur when a control is trying to tell you something. The following real-life example handles one event by raising another.

```
Private Sub Elmo_Click(Button As Integer, Shift As
Integer, X As Single, Y As Single)
    If X = BellyButton.Left And
 Y = BellyButton.Top Then
        RaiseEvent Tickle
    End If
End Sub
```

This code determines if Elmo's bellybutton has been clicked. If so, it raises the tickle event. The Tickle handler is shown below.

```
Private Sub Elmo_Tickle ()
    Dim TickleCount as Integer

    TickleCount = TickleCount + 1
    If TickleCount = 1 Then
        Message "Tee hee hee. That tickles."
    ElseIf TickleCount = 2 Then
        Message "Knock it off, pal. I said it tickles."
    Else
        MsgBox "DIE YOU *#%^ %^@%*#!"
        TickleCount = 0
    End If
End Sub
```

Incidentally, this early version of the Elmo algorithm was quickly pulled off the market.

The Visual Basic help files describe the events raised by each control. Table 2 lists several events not found in the help files.

Table 2   Events

Year	Description
15,000,000,000 BC	Big Bang leads to eventual creation of Dilbert.
1968	Gary Puckett and the Union Gap begins string of hits by releasing the same song over and over again.
1969	Man first walks on moon.
1860	Man first walks on linoleum.
1990	Windows 3.0 forever changes the way we think about flaky software

1994	Mr. Bunny gains his special powers when a lab rabbit at the Massachusetts Institute of Technology is bitten by a crazed computer science major on a Jolt Cola jag.
1995	Windows 95 forever changes the way we think about flaky software.
1996	A new computer language overcomes the drawbacks of C++ and leads to peace in Bosnia and the Middle East.
1997	Visual Basic 5.0 forever changes the way we think about flaky software.
????	The millennium problem is solved when the government bans use of dates.

Building ActiveX Controls

"Just as I suspected," said Mr. Bunny. "It's a secret missile base!"

Mr. Bunny had discovered what many engineers have known all along. Deep inside the ActiveX architecture were row on row of armed missiles. The adventurous rabbit and his befuddled friend had fallen through a missile silo! (See the sidebar titled **Weeeee!**) They now stood in an underground cavern filled with blinking lights and glowing monitors and eerie plumbing.

"This place is scary!" said Farmer Jake. Petey Parachute and Larry Lariat climbed back into Mr. Bunny's pack, and Farmer Jake wished he could join them.

It wasn't the creepy shadows or the flashing consoles that scared the farmer. It wasn't the hum of machinery or the ghostly swish of pneumatic tubes. It wasn't even the menacing missiles towering in the murky distance that caused the farmer's britches to twitch.

There, next to a nearby console, reflecting the ghostly light of the cavern, was a cute little balloon animal. What sort of a madman would create such a thing?

It didn't take long to find out. Something was moving in the shadows!

"Who is zere?" came a man's voice, with a hint of accent.

"I'm Mr. Bunny," called Mr. Bunny. "And this is my associate, Farmer Jake."

"Have you come to inspect ze plumbing?" The voice was closer.

"We're here to learn about ActiveX," said Mr. Bunny.

A small grayish man in a lab coat stepped out of the shadows.

"Ah yes. Everyone wants to know about ActiveX," said the man, pronouncing ActiveX more like 'OCX'.

"I am Professor Oops," said the little man. "You have come at a busy time. I have many objects to create, and miles to go before I yield time to the Windows scheduler."

Think of Professor Oops as a funny looking little man who, even with his head of wild white hair, was not much taller than Mr. Bunny. Note that numerous colored balloons hung limply from his lab coat pockets. He even had a balloon tucked behind his ear! When a beeper sounded on one of the consoles, Professor Oops shuffled over and pulled a balloon from his lab coat and inflated it in a single breath. This behavior is typical of the Professor.

BEEP!

The professor opened a pneumatic tube and popped in the balloon. SQUIPPP! The balloon was sucked right up the tube, and a little counter clicked: Over 2,000,000,000 served.

"But where are we?" asked Farmer Jake.

"Silly boy, you are in ze Object Factory," said the professor.

It was true. Half-built objects were everywhere. Object parts were stacked in the shadows, and the floor was littered with code fragments and balloon bits. Software bugs scuttled here and there in the shadows.

Professor Oops picked a shiny gizmo off a shelf and inflated a balloon right around it like a wrapper, a useful technique when converting legacy code.[7] Farmer Jake noticed an insect trapped in the balloon with the gizmo, but there was no time for testing.

"My work is never done," said the professor.

SQUIPPP! The balloon disappeared up another tube, and Farmer Jake thought he heard the distant sound of an application crashing in the forest.

"But I just want to know how to make an ActiveX control," moaned the old farmer.

"Well why didn't you say so!" said the professor. "Allow me to demonstrate." For this example, imagine the professor pulling several uninflated balloons from his lab coat.

"First you start with your constituent controls," he said, stretching each balloon in turn to make them easier to inflate.

In Visual Basic, simply choose the required controls from the toolbox. Stretch the control to the desired size, as shown by Larry Lariat (please refer to Chapter 4).

"Then you pump up their properties."

The professor quickly inflated each balloon.

Setting properties in Visual Basic is just as easy. Click on the control, then set the desired properties in the Properties Window. (A number of common properties were discussed in Chapter 4.) Some controls support property pages. These controls will have a property named Custom. Double-click the Custom property to

---

7.   Bubble gum may be used if your schedule is tight.

63

bring up the control's Property Page dialog box. Each property page will have a separate tab in the dialog. Note that you can add property pages to your own ActiveX controls. The easiest way to do this is by using the Property Page Wizard. First you should complete the overall design of your control and implement all of its properties. Then select Property Page Wizard from the add-in dialog...

"Excuse me," said Professor Oops. "I was in ze middle of a demo here."

Oh, sorry.

The professor continued. "Then you tie your constituent controls together with a little glue code..."

With a tweak here and a squeak there, the professor twisted the balloons together, as shown in Figure ЖЖ.ЖЖ.

"And there you have it!"

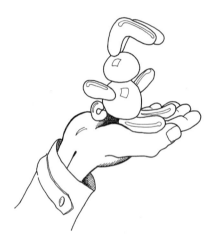

Figure ЖЖ.ЖЖ: ActiveX Control

"It looks just like you, Mr. Bunny!" cried Farmer Jake in surprise.

Another beeper sounded on one of the consoles. Professor Oops scurried over and fiddled with some knobs. And with a SQUINK, the little balloon object was sucked up into a pneumatic tube.

Buzzers buzzed and beepers beeped, and Professor Oops excused himself to pull more levers and press more buttons and shuttle more balloon animals from tube to tube to tube. Farmer Jake just wasn't used to this kind of technology! Things sure have changed since my first cabbage patch, he thought.

Mr. Bunny had other concerns.

Those missiles towering ominously in the shadows…what could they mean? Were they part of ActiveX?

An unusual console caught the rabbit's eye. It was different than the others. Mr. Bunny took a closer look. It seemed to be some sort of navigational targeting system, and it showed a vaguely familiar map.

Farmer Jake called out from a nearby control panel. "What do you suppose this big red button is for?"

But Mr. Bunny did not hear him. The map looked so familiar. An island country…

The farmer reached for the button...

"I've got it!" said Mr. Bunny. "I know where the missiles are aimed!"

…and old Jake pushed the button down.

"JAVA!" cried the rabbit.

BRR_RUMBLE!!!

The missiles thundered to life!

Summary

- Visual Basic 5.0 provides a powerful programming environment for creating little elves.
- You can earn extra money by making balloon animals at birthday parties and company board meetings.
- Don't click on any buttons unless you know what they do.

Exercises

1. Click on Visual Basic's buttons to see what they do.

2. Optimize the following Visual Basic code:
   n = 1

3. Discuss the mating habits of the North American fresh water salmon.

Additional Reading

- *Bunny Cakes.* Rosemary Wells.
- *Rabbit's Good News.* Ruth Lecher Bornstein.
- *The Runaway Bunny.* Margaret Wise Brown.
- *PC Roadkill.* Michael Hyman.

Chapter 6

The explosion of the Internet has scattered debris across the World Wide Web and raised questions not even dreamed of just three or four minutes ago. Will computer networking ever catch on? Does the deployment of ActiveX controls via the Internet indicate a policy of mutually assured destruction? Can Java really produce a magic beanstalk, or is Jack just the village idiot after all?

Since this book is not a fairy tale, Chapter 6 ignores Java. All the better to focus on ActiveX and the fate of our talking bunny rabbit.

Delivering the Goods

Farmer Jake and Mr. Bunny ran for the nearest missile as it hissed and fumed and rumbled to life. Far overhead the silo doors slid open, dotting the darkness with circles of light.

"Hurry," cried Mr. Bunny. "We're going for a ride!"

The Setup Wizard

The Setup Wizard (Figure -·····.·----.) allows you to "wave a magic wand" over your Visual Basic "application", so that it can be delivered over the Internet.

To use the Setup Wizard, follow these easy steps.

Step 1: Locate and run the Setup Wizard using the procedure described for Running Visual Basic in Chapter 4. Pay no attention to the man behind the curtain.

Step 2: Locate your VB project. If someone asks if you need help, tell them "No thanks, I'm just browsing."

Step 3: Put on a large hat made of fruit.

Step 4: Mark your component as safe by clicking the Safety button. If your component contains malicious code that will damage the user's system in order to bring imagined glory to your twisted ego, then you can skip this step.

Step 5: Click Cancel.

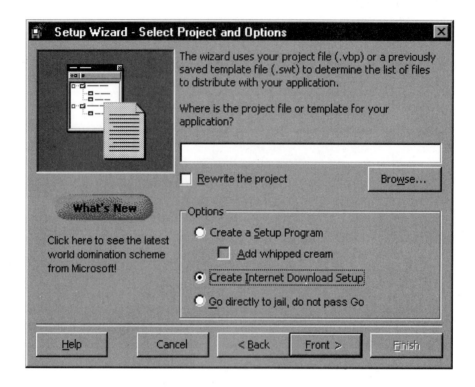

Figure ⁻ ⁽⁾ ⁻ : Setup Wizard

The Setup Wizard creates a compressed .CAB file that can be downloaded via the World Wide Web. If the file is not sufficiently compressed, you may need to step on it some.

Deploying the Control

Mr. Bunny opened a hatch on the side of the missile, and he and Farmer Jake quickly jumped inside.

VROOOSHHH!

They were airborne!

Farmer Jake felt his body tingle with the sensory static of undifferentiated cyberspace. No, he was just sitting on his rake.

The pair peered out a portal at the scene below. The missile was climbing through a matrix of interconnected jet trails above a vast sea of hexadecimal digits. The ebb and flow of ever-changing hyperlinks cast a restless moiré pattern of shadows on the rabbit's bifocals. *Tee hee hee*, giggled Farmer Jake at the sight of the cute little bunny.

The colorful content of a million web pages rushed past as they ascended through shifting data planes. They saw the ten most popular Web sites.

0. *www.shave-and-a-haircut.com*
   Barbers online. Four chairs, no waiting.
1. *www.recipes.com/10W-40.htm*
   Cooking with motor oil.
2. *www.screeeech.com*
   Visitors remotely control a New York City taxicab.
3. *www.hottrash.com*
   Order a dumpster heater so your trash can stink in the winter, too.
4. *www.bugcam.com*
   Live images of a bug zapper in Missoula, Montana.
5. *www.philatelick.com*
   View the backside of a postage stamp.
6. *www.Church_of_Eddie.com*
   Religious cult awaits the second coming of Eddie Munster.
7. *www.wwwwwwwwwwwwwwwwwwwwwwww.com*
   Storage site for all those w's used on the Internet.
8. *www.connoisseur.com/ABTA.htm*
   Home page of the American Brick Taster Association.
9. *www.microsoft.com*
   World's largest collection of toenail clippings.

Mr. Bunny remembered the targeting system back in the cavern. There was no telling what this missile would do when it reached its destination, but he sure wasn't going to hang around to find out.

"This missile isn't safe," he said. "We must jump!" And with his powerful hind legs, Mr. Bunny kicked open the portal and pushed Farmer Jake into a binary cloud of fuzzy logic.

WEEEEEE!

Mr. Bunny followed right behind, and Farmer Jake caught hold of him. The clever rabbit punched some buttons on his pocket protector while Farmer Jake held on for his life.

VROOOM!

Mr. Bunny's rucksack shot columns of fire. It was a jet pack! The two Internet explorers were flying through the World Wide Web.

"I don't have enough power for both of us," said Mr. Bunny. "We're going to splash down."

WOOOSHHH!

Out of his rucksack popped Ducky Tub Toy.

"Surf's up!" cried Ducky.

SPLOOSH!

SPLOOSH!

SPLOOSH!

A farmer, a rabbit, and a duck dropped out of the sky and splashed into an ocean of data.

Cabinet Files

The Internet setup for your control can provide all the needed objects, or some support files such as MSVBVM50.DLL can be downloaded separately. In either case, Mr. Bunny and Farmer Jake climbed onto Ducky Tub Toy's back. Farmer Jake noticed that debris floated all around them.

"Was there a shipwreck?" he asked.

"These are cabinet files," explained Mr. Bunny. "They contain the ActiveX controls and all dependent files required for the controls to operate."

A cabinet file floated nearby. Farmer Jake opened a drawer and took a look inside. It contained the Visual Basic runtime DLLs, several mysterious Bermuda shorts, and a half dozen stale donuts left over from a corporate staff meeting.

"Land ho!" cried Ducky Tub Toy.

"These cabinets are a stroke of luck," said Mr. Bunny. "We'll need them to get ashore."

Mr. Bunny was right. The first time a system sees a control referenced in a Web page, it will have no idea how to load it. A control's .CAB file contains everything needed for the control to run. But does the .CAB file just wash up on shore by wild coincidence? No, there are now far too many controls for the *coincidence mechanism* to work reliably. Instead, the CODEBASE attribute of the HTML <OBJECT> tag provides the URL of the control. But we're getting ahead of our story. Farmer Jake was trying on some Bermuda shorts on top of his overalls when suddenly the water heaved and a giant serpent broke the surface!

The little tub toy was swamped. Farmer and Bunny overboard!

"It's a Web crawler sniffing around for useful URLs," gurgled Mr. Bunny. "Swim to one of the cabinet files. The next section will explain the technical details!"

"See you on shore!" called Ducky.

Farmer Jake held onto a cabinet and rode the breakers onto the strangest beach that he had ever seen.

HTML

Before we familiarize ourselves with what happens to Mr. Bunny and Farmer Jake and Ducky Tub Toy, we will examine some of the highlights of HTML (*HyperText Markup Language*).

HTML is the language spoken by a tribe of headhunters near the source of the Nile. It has proven useful for creating web pages and frenzied pygmy dance rituals. It is a simple language that can be edited with tools such as EDLIN, vi, or the air traffic control system at O'Hare International Airport.

The main feature of HTML is the *tag* (the authentic pygmy pronunciation uses a clucking sound made near the back of the throat). A tag is a command that marks headings, paragraphs, lists, images, contaminated beef, and so on.

Here is a sample heading tag:

```
<H1>   HELP! I'M TRAPPED IN THIS WEB PAGE!   </H1>
```

This tag marks the enclosed string as heading level 1. There are six possible heading levels (approximately **H1** through **H5**). In the future thousands of heading levels may be possible.

Of course, there is more to a web page than headings. You'll want to use pictures, and lots of them! The more cluttered your web page, the more time visitors will spend there trying to figure it out.

The image tag allows an image file to be specified:

```
<IMG SRC="filename.gif">
```

Here SRC is an attribute of the IMG tag. It specifies the case sensitive name of the image file. (By the way, "filename.gif" is just a placeholder for your own file name. Your own image files will be called "Skippy.")

Note that tags are *not* case sensitive. Thus IMG SRC can be written as Img src or iMg Src or imG src or iMG Src or img sRc or Img srC or ImG src or ImG src or Img Src or Img sRc or Img srC or IMG src or Img Src or Img sRc or

ImG srC or IMG Src or iMG sRC or IMG srC or IMG SRc or ImG SRC, for example.

 The symbols '<' and '>' must always be capitalized.

To include an ActiveX control in a web page, use the <OBJECT> tag. Remember the class identifiers that Mr. Bunny entered into the Windows Registry? Here they are again! Can you find the mistake? (Hint: why bother?)

```
<OBJECT>
ID="Mr.Bunny"
CLASSID="CLSID: 16014620-d12e-11d0-bb13-0000c0cf6ecf"
CODEBASE="MrBunny.CAB#version=1,0,0,0">
</OBJECT>

<OBJECT>
ID="Farmer.Jake"
CLASSID="CLSID: 16014621-d12e-11d0-bb13-0000c0cf6ecf"
CODEBASE="FarmerJake.CAB#version=1,0,0,0">
</OBJECT>
```

The next section will serve to make this even more confusing.

On the Same Page

Ducky Tub Toy waddled ashore, and watched as two cabinets washed up on the beach in a spray of foam and .WAV files.

CRASH! went the waves.

SMASH! went the cabinets.

And out hopped Mr. Bunny and Farmer Jake.

The sand felt funny under Farmer Jake's feet. Why, it wasn't sand at all!

It was a lime green shag carpet!

But it was more than the shabby shag that offended the delicate sensibilities of the old hoe jockey. The beach displayed a tasteless mix of period decor. Waves splashed an early American Barcalounger, barnacles encrusted a Louis XIV beanbag chair, and under an Art Deco sun the exuberant ornamentation of a Renaissance tilt-table printer stand clashed with the enigmatic painting of dogs playing poker circa Woolworth's 1980.

Farmer Jake tried to make out illegible fluorescent yellow skywriting against the red floral wallpaper of the sky, but it was no use. He could feel the web page sucking the will to live from his retinas. "This place looks worse than Bessie's stall in the barn," he said.

"Quack," said Ducky in disgust, and climbed back into Mr. Bunny's pack.

"Years ago the desktop publishing boom spawned a similar glut of tacky newsletters, wedding invitations, and death certificates," said the cute little cotton-tail. "Today a plethora of web development tools let professionals create web pages any parent would be proud to hang on the refrigerator."

Figure - ⋯⋯.⋯--- : Farmer Jake and Mr. Bunny visit a web page

WHOOPS!

The old farmer almost fell over. He had stepped on a banana peel.

"Must be a SLIP connection," said Mr. Bunny.

Just then the pair heard the sound of brassy Mexican music floating on the breeze.

"Mr. Bunny!" called a familiar voice.

"Smitty!" Mr. Bunny called back.

Sure enough, it was the little lawn gnome and all his friends, all decked out in Mexican hats and sparkling sequined suits. The sounds of trumpet and violin and guitar filled the air. They were a Mariachi band!

It was a multimedia beach party!

"Oh, boy!" grinned Farmer Jake. But he quickly lost his smile when a shrill alarm blared, drowning out the Mexican rhythms.

What was going on? Everything seemed to be happening at once!

Lights flashed. A siren screamed. The band stopped playing. Police cars were everywhere. Farmer Jake and Mr. Bunny were surrounded!

Two burly police officers were heading right toward them.

"Halt!" cried one of the officers. "This is a restricted area. You can't play in our sandbox!"

"The user must have specified a high-security setting," whispered Mr. Bunny. "We have to get out of here."

But they could barely move!

Farmer Jake tugged on his leg and managed a jerky step. Mr. Bunny seemed to be having the same problem. Then Farmer Jake noticed this was an animated web page. Palm trees swayed to and fro, but something was wrong. The trees blinked back and forth like a cheap neon sign. Even the breeze seemed to stop and start in fits.

"This animation isn't very smooth," said Mr. Bunny. "Too many animated controls will bog down even the fastest machines. It's best to use only the lowest common denominator elements on your Web pages to assure they will run on all systems. A blank page is ideal."

GRRR_WOOF! WOOF!

A ferocious-looking dog was charging toward them!

"Get 'em, Bowser," shouted one of the officers.

"We must go or we'll wind up in the bit bucket!" said the rabbit.

"But I can barely move!" cried Farmer Jake.

"Nothing runs very fast in this environment," said Mr. Bunny. But the clever rabbit was always ready. Once again he reached into his magic rucksack.

"Stop!" called the police.

"GRRR_WOOF," barked Bowser.

FWOOOP! went Mr. Bunny's rucksack.

And out popped Buster Gasbag!

"Howdy, Mr. Bunny!" said Buster.

"Get us out of here," cried the rabbit.

Bowser was almost upon them!

GRRR_WOOF! WOOF!

The farmer and the rabbit hopped into Buster's basket, and Buster puffed up his cheeks, and up up and away they flew.

Security Considerations

Many people are concerned about the security of ActiveX controls. Once on your machine, an ActiveX control has full access to your system. If you are not careful, it could delete your hard drive, corrupt your politicians, or order an unauthorized pizza.

Fortunately there are some solutions to the security problem.

First, the designer of the control marks the control as safe only if the control is actually safe to use. It is almost unthinkable that someone with hostile intentions would lie about something like this.

Next, most pizza shops call back to confirm your phone number before delivery.

And finally, as you've seen, any Bowser can be configured to chase unauthorized personnel off the beach.

The police stood on the shag carpet beach and shook their fists while Bowser jumped and yelped and waves crashed against the tacky furniture. But Farmer and Buster and Bunny were all safely out of reach.

"Take us away from here, Buster," said Mr. Bunny. "I think Farmer Jake has had enough."

See figure -⋯.⋯--.

And as they floated past a giant toolbar in the sky, Mr. Bunny once again took Petey the Peashooter from his rucksack and DINGED a button labelled "Home."

Far below Stevie the Status Bar said: *Contacting www.mrbunny.com...*

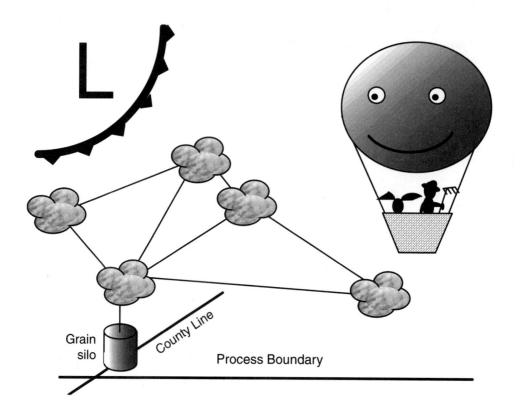

Figure - ⋯⋅.⋯⋅ - : "Take us home," said Mr. Bunny.

Final Thoughts

Well, we've covered a lot of ground. You now have an inside view of ActiveX. You've learned all about the Common Object Model, you've seen how to design and implement an ActiveX control using Visual Basic 5.0, and you've seen your controls travel across the World Wide Web only to be denied access by the browser's security settings. Lastly, you have gained an understanding of Mr. Bunny and Farmer Jake, who have just returned to the farmer's back porch and are sipping lemonade as the sun goes down.

"Well that was more fun than the time Aunt Agnes lost her glass eye in the fruit salad," said Farmer Jake. "It's too bad it all had to end so soon."

"We need to save something for the sequel," said Mr. Bunny mysteriously.

The old farmer was puzzled, but he knew that for now this was all the information he would get from the furry little *Oryctolagus cuniculus*.

So the two sat in silence. Farmer Jake fiddled with his favorite garden rake, and Mr. Bunny lapped his lemonade with a pink little tongue. The evening breeze was cool, and carried the promise of new software projects to come.

"Pappy?" called a chorus of wee voices from inside the house.

"Come on out, kids," said Farmer Jake.

Out trotted three tikes in overalls. They looked just like a trio of miniature Farmer Jakes.

"This is Jake1 and Jake2 and Jake3," said the farmer.

"Hi Mr. Bunny!" said Jake1.

"Hi Mr. Bunny!" said Jake2.

"Hi Mr. Bunny!" said Jake3.

Just then the house began to BRRR_UMBLE.

Was it another missile launch?

"Don't worry," said Farmer Jake. "It's just the wife wonderin' where I been all day. Come on kids. I'll tell you a bedtime story about the latest component technologies."

"Oh boy!" said Jake1.

"Oh boy!" said Jake2.

"Oh boy!" said Jake3.

The old farmer rose to go inside. "I'm comin', Bessie," he said, and turned to say goodbye to his funny fuzzy friend.

The sun had gone down, but Mr. Bunny's glasses reflected another light, the reddish glow of mushrooming clouds from the general direction of Indonesia.

"Sleep tight," said the little rabbit with a wink.

Appendix A

Mr. Bunny Answers Your Letters

Dear Mr. Bunny: My code doesn't work. What should I do?
- FJ

Mr. Bunny replies: Very often code doesn't work the first time. Try running it again.

Dear Mr. Bunny: My allergies seem to act up whenever I try to return a value from a function.
- NS

Mr. Bunny replies: The pollen count of return values is very high this year. Try wrapping your monitor in cellophane.

Dear Mr. Bunny: I recently had to maintain some poorly written code, and now my doctor says I need glasses. Can this be related?
- RP

Mr. Bunny replies: Failing eyesight is often the brain's only defense against poorly written code. Take frequent breaks. I recommend a one hour break every thirty seconds.

Dear Mr. Bunny: I'm working on the next killer application, an integrated software suite for keeping track of recipes. Do you think this is a good idea?
- LS

Mr. Bunny replies: Don't waste your time. For years computer scientists have searched for a solution to the "recipe problem"; no suitable algorithm has been found.

Dear Mr. Bunny: My project leader's birthday is coming soon, and I'd like to sing him a nice little song parody. Any ideas?
- SV

Mr. Bunny replies: Try singing this to the tune of Happy Birthday:

ActiveX ActiveX
ActiveX ActiveX
ActiveX ActiveX
ActiveX ActiveX

Dear Mr. Bunny: I enjoyed your recent article about programming and stuff, but I must offer a few complaints. Your hashed array tree algorithm exhibits inefficiencies. Since the bifurcated bologna approach relies on searching the generated combinations for duplicates, the time complexity can be shown to approach N squared. If a large number of involutions is expected, I generally eschew the technique.
- GS

Mr. Bunny replies: I have no idea what you're talking about.

Appendix B

Answers to exercises

Chapter 2

1   2

Chapter 3

Chapter 4

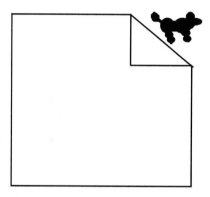

Chapter 5

The Visual Basic code:

```
n = 1
```

can be optimized as follows:

```
If n <> 1 Then
    n = 1
End If
```

It is also acceptable to rewrite the code in C:

```
n = 1;
```

Appendix C

Sound Effect Definitions

The following header file defines the sound effects used in this book. Include this header before compiling.

```
#ifndef sounds_h
#define sounds_h

#define BRRR_RUMBLE    0x001
#define DING           0x002
#define FOOP           0x003
#define FWIPP          0x004
#define FWOOOP         0x005
#define GRRR_WOOF      0x006
#define SPLOOSH        0x007
#define SQUINK         0x008
#define SQUIPPP        0x009
#define VROOOM         0x00A
#define VROOOSHHH      0x00B
#define WEEEEEE        0x00C
#define WHOOP          0x00D
#define WHOOPS         0x00E
#define WHOOSH         0x00F
#define WOOF           0x00G
#define ZING           0x00H
#define CRASH          0x00I
#define SMASH          0x00J

#endif // sounds_h
```

Index

—A—

ActiveX
  AUTOEXEC.BAT, 29
  Bermuda shorts, 72
  C++, 15, 16, 20, 37, 48, 55
  Cabinet Files, 72
  Class Identifiers, 30
  CLSCTX_INPROC_HANDLER, 22
  CLSCTX_INPROC_SERVER, 22
  CLSCTX_LOCAL_SERVER, 22
  CLSID, 22, 30, 32, 74
  CoCreateInstance, 21, 22
  COM, 4, 11, 13, 17, 18, 20
  component-based software, 5, 6, 8
  components, 5, 7, 8, 11, 14, 45
  ComSpec, 28
  CONFIGI.SYS, 29
  crusty old cropper, 29
  Ducky Tub Toy, 72, 74
  Elmo, 61
  Events, 60
  Farmer Jake, x, xi, xii, 5, 6, 8, 11, 13, 14, 15, 16, 17, 19, 20, 23, 27, 28, 29, 30, 31, 32, 33, 37, 42, 43, 44, 46, 47, 48, 49, 50, 51, 52, 53, 60, 62, 63, 64, 65, 69, 70, 71, 72, 73, 74, 75, 76, 77, 78, 79
FARPROC, 15
FileSystem, 28, 29, 30
Foo, 14, 15
GetProcAddress, 15, 19, 20
HTML, 72, 73
IFlyingEnchilada, 23
information bunny trail, x
IUnknown, 13, 22
LoadLibrary, 19, 20
Methods, 60

Mr. Bunny, x, xi, xii, xiii, 3, 5, 6, 8, 11, 13, 14, 15, 16, 17, 18, 19, 20, 21, 22, 23, 27, 28, 29, 30, 31, 32, 33, 37, 46, 47, 48, 49, 50, 51, 52, 53, 60, 62, 64, 65, 69, 70, 71, 72, 74, 75, 76, 77, 78, 79, 81, 89
n, xiv, 65, 84
Object Factory, 63
OLE, 4, 5, 13, 18
organic refuse, 29
pixel, 4
Planned Obsolescence, 29
Property Page, 64
Registry, xii, 19, 27, 28, 29, 30, 32, 33, 74
Security, 30
Setup Wizard, 69, 70
Smith, 96de0250-cbc1-11d0-bb0b-0000c0cf6ecf, 19
SYSTEM.INI, 29
Underpinnings of, 13
virtual functions, 15, 16
Visual Basic, xii, 11, 29, 35, 37, 38, 39, 40, 42, 43, 46, 49, 50, 51, 52, 53, 55, 58, 63, 69, 72, 78
Vtable, 16, 17
weird stuff, xi
WHATEVER.INI, 29
WIN.INI. *See* ActiveX
Windows 95, 29
Windows API and, 15
Winnemucca, Nevada., 17
AUTOEXEC.BAT. *See* ActiveX

—B—

Bermuda shorts. *See* Active X
Bunny. *See* Mr. Bunny

—C—

C++. *See* ActiveX
Cabinet Files. *See* ActiveX
Class Identifiers. *See* ActiveX
CLSCTX_INPROC_HANDLER. *See* ActiveX
CLSCTX_INPROC_SERVER. *See* ActiveX
CLSCTX_LOCAL_SERVER. *See* ActiveX
CLSID. *See* ActiveX
CoCreateInstance. *See* ActiveX
COM. See ActiveX
Component Object Model. See COM
component-based software. *See* ActiveX
components. *See* ActiveX
ComSpec. *See* ActiveX
CONFIGI.SYS. *See* ActiveX
crusty old cropper. *See* ActiveX

—D—

Ducky Tub Toy. *See* ActiveX

—E—

Elmo. *See* ActiveX
Events. *See* ActiveX

—F—

FARPROC. *See* ActiveX
FileSystem. *See* ActiveX
Foo. *See* ActiveX

—G—

GetProcAddress. *See* ActiveX

—H—

HTML. *See* ActiveX

—I—

Index, 86
information bunny trail. *See* ActiveX
IUnknown. *See* ActiveX

—K—

kidney stone. *See a doctor*

—L—

LoadLibrary. *See* ActiveX

—M—

Methods. *See* ActiveX
Mr. Bunny. *See* ActiveX

—N—

n. *See* ActiveX

—O—

Object Factory. *See* ActiveX
OLE. *See* ActiveX
organic refuse. *See* ActiveX

—P—

pixel. *See* ActiveX
Planned Obsolescence. *See* ActiveX
Property Page. *See* ActiveX

—R—

Registry. *See* ActiveX

—S—

Security. *See* ActiveX
Setup Wizard. *See* ActiveX
Smith, 96de0250-cbc1-11d0-bb0b-
    0000c0cf6ecf. *See* ActiveX
SYSTEM.INI. *See* ActiveX

—U—

Underpinnings of ActiveX. *See* ActiveX,
    Underpinnings of

—V—

virtual functions. *See* ActiveX
Visual Basic. *See* ActiveX
Vtable. *See* ActiveX

—W—

weird stuff. *See* ActiveX
WHATEVER.INI. *See* ActiveX
Windows 95. *See* ActiveX
Windows API. *See* ActiveX, Windows API and
Winnemucca, Nevada. *See* ActiveX

About the Author

Carlton Egremont III has lived a privileged life. His paternal grandfather made the family fortune with the invention of those things that separate groceries at the checkout counter, and baby Carlton arrived amid the fabulous opulence of the famous Egremont estate, where he enjoyed a brief period of celebrity as the world's youngest baby.

As a child young Master Egremont was affectionately nicknamed "Vinnie the Slug" by his mother. He dreamed of writing a book about Microsoft Windows. This innocent dream resulted in many visits to a drive-thru psychiatrist, where Carlton would lie on the back seat of the family limousine and explain his visions to a plastic clown head.

As a young adult, Carlton Egremont III left the estate to live a playboy lifestyle, surrounded as he was by magazines in a three-room flat in New Jersey. It was here he discovered a passion for agriculture and raised his first crop of organic poison ivy.

He completed his first book at the age of 27. Critics argued that although he had colored outside the lines, it nonetheless could not be considered original work. The book is out of print.

Mr. Egremont is now back in favor with his family. The Egremont dynasty is proud of the Mr. Bunny series, and knighthood could be in the future for the author, who has sent in a cereal box top and hopes to win the contest.

Mr. Egremont is currently daydreaming about his next book. He still has trouble coloring inside the lines.

Praise Page for Mr. Bunny

"No one explains COM better than Carlton Egremont III."
Don Box, COM Guy, Not affiliated with Microsoft Corp.

"What a terrible thing to have lost one's mind. Or not to have a mind at all.
How true that is."
*Vice President Dan Quayle winning friends while speaking to
the United Negro College Fund*

"Nobody says nothing better, with more precision and insight!"
Chief Scientist of Moonsphere, Inc.

"...hilarious....Egremont nails the how-to book conventions."
Hillary Rettig
VARBusiness
www.varbusiness.com

"This is just about the funniest piece of technical literature I've ever read."
Charlie Kindel
Microsoft DCOM Developer's Mailing List

"...extremely humorous...masterfully combines techno-terms with baby
talk."
Computer Literacy Bookshops Online
www.clbooks.com

"...cheap at half the price."
Keith Dawson
Tasty Bits from the Technology Front
www.tbtf.com

But Seriously

The author wishes to thank Bob and Rick Treitman of Softpro Software and Books for their early adoption of Mr. Bunny. They were quick to recognize that a talking rabbit has no place in a bookstore for professionals, yet their store in Burlington, Massachusetts, was the first to carry this book. Please don't hold that against them.